Distribution of, and further information about the Messages of Love as given by Jesus, through the two Patricks, can be obtained from:

An Invitation to Love Jesus
Sacred Heart House of Prayer
46 James Street
Cookstown
Co. Tyrone
Northern Ireland
BT8O 8LT
Tel: 028 867 66377
Fax: 028 867 62247

PUBLISHING

Published by JPP Publishing
ISBN 1-904495-12-5

Dedicated to the
Most Sacred Heart of Jesus

Introduction

In keeping with the theme of Love that Jesus presents to the world through the Messages of Love, we present this book of the beautiful Lovesongs of Jesus. These were given at various times during a period of fourteen years.

The Songs or Poems speak of a Love for the soul and Jesus is the Lover who speaks them. They speak directly to the deepest part of the soul of spiritual Love and of spiritual marriage. In them, Jesus has shown a side of Himself that is not often seen. He cries out in an almost abject fear of losing the soul to the enemy and often speaks of the Pain that He feels in wooing it.

He comes like an ethereal spirit to cast bounteous Words and Gifts and jewels of great spiritual value unto us in order to win us over. His Love is the great prize that He presents to us and it is only the beginning of what seems like a roller coaster ride into the unknown. He is the jealous Lover that gathers the soul to Him to cast the self in it away and speaks of the promise in store for it.

His caress is the kiss of a butterfly wing as it softly embraces the air in silent flight; a feather alighting upon the ground in an inaudible whisper. His Love is the promise of Eternity and the dizzy heights of ecstasy when it pierces through the mind and heart and all things physical to break and tear into the soul's house. For He does not knock, He shatters. With one look, embrace, touch, He holds captive the soul, which is His unprejudiced objective, to enfold it and impress it upon His Heart, to scar it and wound it and to Love tenderly the soul.

These Words are rich in beauty, simplicity and Love and are spoken to any soul who will allow them to penetrate fully, as the rain drenches. Read and behold the Love of the Most Sacred Heart of Jesus. These are not Words, these are Love.

From Juan De La Cruz

Oh Divine Night,
Shown only
In the Light
Of Darkness.
Listen to the teachings, children,
Of the Night.
For much is foretold
In the Words.
That from which life absconds,
Becomes the enemy.
For dreams and thoughts
Of self,
Shalt run
And break away
When the gentle, tranquil breezes
Begin to blow, of many facets.
And abstract thoughts
Dance around
And life and self and all
Is thrown headlong

Upon the Fire of Intensity,
Of the Night.
Burning
With caresses,
Pain,
And consuming all.
For none is needed now,
None will be accepted
Upon the threshold of the Chamber
Over which the Lover will carry
You.
And there shalt you be taken
For (what Raptures)
The frenzy of the Night.
Upon Flowered Breast
Shalt thou be wedded.
His Love has fallen
For the comely look of thee.
And thou shalt rise
And rise again:
And thou shalt leave
Thy house in darkness,
In Night.
And thou shalt know the Pain

That Love endures
For thou and all.
In the blackest Night,
Not sorrow, but Love.
And He shalt fall for thee;
For thy death.
And He shalt look for thee;
And in thee He shalt look
For nothing
And nothing.
Hiddenness shalt claim thee
And be their mother.
A vast, yet, tiny darkness
Shalt thou behold.
And Night shalt fall upon thee;
In deepest, blackness darkness,
For Light hath gone.
And for innerness shalt Light appear
Each time thy house is left.
Look and look again,
For, Oh what consummation
Shalt endure
For thee and thee and thee.
And Living, shalt thou know.

The Flame that Burns
And Cauterises.
And the Night
And the Light
Is Jesus.
And thee – His brides –
Caught up in Love
That does not expend,
And is not spent
Upon the Flowers of the Dawn.

For Life and Life alone
Shalt thou have,
In death.
And this death is New Life, my children.
It is Him, who Loves thee,
And tires not of Loving thee.

Poem of Love from Jesus

Poems and songs I sing
Upon the souls of My Love.
Come close,
Let Me be the guide, soul of My Love.
Oh sweet and tender Love
I pour upon you
I call, I guide,
I look, I Love and hunger for you.
Oh gentle caress; consumed in Love.
Our Hearts become one.
Oh sweet caress,
My soul, My love,
It is I, your Jesus, who calls.
I whisper to your love.
Oh soul of My Love,
Listen, come,
Run to Me.
I will sweep you away in Arms of Love.
Ah, how My Heart races as I think of the soul
that I Love.

I Love you.

Yes, it is you, My child, I address you as you read these, My Words of Love. Read them many times in the silence of your prayer. You shall know the Peace and Love of My Most Sacred Heart. I Love you, My child.

To joy, My little ones,
For she is indeed your kin
And Mine.
Take joy in your Lord, My children.
The night is indeed long
And the waters dark;
Persist in the journey
I await to greet you.
Many toils in My Love;
Many pains to be felt;
But joy should be your delight.
Do not fear, I say,
Do not fear.
For fear mars the Plan that I have set for you.
Let Me embrace you in My Love,
Let you quench My Thirst.

I crave you;
I crave to welcome your soul into Mine.

In the depths of your spirit I will arise.
Come, calling to Me
Do not fear, My dove.
The night is dark
The journey long
Much pain to be felt,
Do not fear losing control,
Be free.
Fly with Me on the Wings of Love.
Come soar with Me
To pastures green.
The land of milk and honey
Awaits you, My dove.
Do not fret.
Do not worry.
Do not let self draw and tear.
Come, come, run My Bride
I, your All, am near.
Enter into Love,
Enter forth into joy.

See this Heart;
See its Pain,
See its Love.
You have forgotten how to see.
I am your God,
I am your Father.
Call Me
Your Abba.

I will seize you

My son, you are so curious
but it delights Me to answer your questions.
I Love you.
How I wish it were your hand
that would take these Words.
Since you ask, I will tell you.
These are My people
and the thoughts that you have had of them
are My inspirations.
They will come to Me when the time is right.
I, too, am longing for you, My son.
My Life is in you
Though you do not believe.
Forgiveness
Is yours
In Me.
Empty yourself
And be, as you would call,
My plaything.
My dove in the cleft of the rock,

Come out
That I may write on you,
And Love you.
Seize Me
As I will seize you.
I Love you.

Lovesong for My Beloved

Jesus:

My son, embrace Me in your love. Come to Me with love and not fear, for fear has taken its toll upon you in this last while. You have been so afraid that My Words will not penetrate you.

Feel Me now; I am like the soft breeze that touches your face, as you become My parchment that I write upon. I am Loving you. I am driving all fear away, for I must make you strong. I embrace you in My Love.

Tenderness comes to you in the shade of twilight and it Loves you. I envelope you.

Patrick:

I was interrupted during this Message with a comment on Patrick O Kane, who was to take a separate Message, but could not due to an attack. Instead, he wrote a poem of his own to Jesus. As he wrote, Jesus, unknown to Patrick O Kane, was giving me a reply to the poem. This is His reply.

Jesus:

Child, I Love you. Tell your brother not to be afraid to take the Words of Love that I am writing to him. I Love him and wish to display it upon the page of his soul. He is My comely Bride, that I Love.

Fold into Me, My dove, and I will fold Myself into you. Like the shining sun, I will warm you. Let Me write on you these Words of Love for your brother. Let Me write:

Songs, I sing within your soul,
Poems I write upon the delicacy
Of your soul.
I, who am Love,
Write the Words
Upon you,
Marking you with My seal.
I give you, Dark One,
The Treasures of My Heart.
Embrace, then, the Towers of Ivory,
The soft myrrh,
The perfume of your delectable soul.
Words, My son, when given in Spirit

Are Truth, and must be.
These Words, I use your brother's time
To create for you.
They are written in My Blood.
Be still, then, heart of My Heart,
Flesh of My Flesh.
I will bloom you.
I see you, My Bride, I dress you
In many jewels; I give you precious perfumes
To anoint the soul that I Love.
Return My Love
Even though the search for Me is long
And arduous, I call to you.
These are Words of Love;
Let them caress you
And touch you.
Embrace Me, Oh, My Bride,
My love, My star, My sunlight.
Taste Me as I Love you.
I am Jesus, Bridegroom of Patrick.
Behold! This day I pledge it.

Patrick's Poem to Jesus:

Oh, my Lord, my God,
I have fallen.
My soul is wounded;
The battle cries have torn
Me limb from limb.
My Love,
My anger is great; I call
But no sound do I hear.
I am like a wounded animal,
fearful and angry.
My love pulses out,
But my lips rip out.
The One I love
in the distance calls.
I am blinded and cannot find
My Love.
Please come and lift this carcass.
My Love, my Love,
where are You?
Ah, the mist falls.

Is darkness my lot -
Loneliness and despair?
My Love, my Love
My call grows fainter.
Do You not care?
Do You not want to know?
Words but echo and wound so deep.
I long for Your faint caress,
My Love.

These Words are Sweet

Touch my heart, as cold as ice;
Break its hard, worldly hold.
Forgive the piercing tongue,
The viper's bite.
Go, Lord,
Break Your hold.
Your Hand bleeds as I snap
And bite.
No longer try,
This heart won't melt.
My Love, my All.
But are these words just lies?
Does one stab the One he loves?
Darkness comes and falls,
My Lord, my God,
My Love, my All,
My Jesus.
Ah, these words are sweet,
But still I wound so deep,
The One I love.

My Jesus,
Is this love?

Messages of Love

My children of this world, how many Lovesongs must I sing to you, how many beautiful Words must I say to you before you listen? Ah, how this Heart bleeds in its Love for you.

I saw you. You were like a barren land. I stripped you of all the dead and rotting vegetation that was in you. I fertilised your soil with My own Blood and you flourished.

My children, My children, where are you? I call out to you in the pangs of Love, but no sound do I hear.

Do you not realise, My little ones - I Love you; I call you through My Prophets, to return, as I have done many times before in the past. Remember, My people, Israel, mocked and scorned them; and you, My children, do the same once again. I call; My Mother calls, but alas, you do not want to listen.

I Love you, My children; all I desire is to hold you in My Arms and bring you to My Father's

Kingdom, but I cannot force you. See the Truth of My Love before it is too late. You have your free will and I cannot take this away from you. Please listen, children; I Love you. Come.

It is with Love that My Heart burns, for it is the fuel that burns to Love all of mankind. I am the great Lover of all souls and I desire that all souls be with Me for Eternity. Look at the earnestness of My Love. Look at the Fire that burns within this Heart of Mine, as I crave to reveal it to mankind. In this wretched state, man attracts Me, because of the sinful state of helplessness that he is in.

Love Words from Jesus

In the olive grove
I shall plant you;
In the cedars I shall grow you.
I shall tend you with My Love.
I shall make springs come forth
From barren rock,
To feed you and keep you.

You shall be the choicest of all
Within My Garden.

And I shall honour you;
I shall give you many jewels to wear,
For your beauty to Me is comely.
I shall court you as My Bride
And give you many Gifts.
Your eyes, I have gazed upon
And found beauty there.
They have touched My Heart.

You shall be the choicest of all
Within My House.

Look to the sun;
I have risen it for you
And it speaks of My Love for you.
My Light, to guide your way,
Shines forth through it.
My Light is the shoes that you wear
To keep you from stumbling in the dark;
And My Light is the crown
That I place upon your head.
For I have taken you
And crushed you like the grape
And took from you all that is good
To make choice wine.
I poured into you My Love.
And you delighted My Heart.

I give you the earth to set under your feet,
I have filled it with good things
For your pleasure.
I grant to you the wind,
To cool your face in the hot sun,

For you are Mine;
I have created you and formed you
So that I could Love you.
And joy is Mine to see you come;
To see your comely face.

Look, before you I set a feast,
Choice wines and finest meats.
Gifts I place upon this table I have set,
Abundant spices to your taste;
And you shall eat your fill,
For you, Oh Israel, I have chosen
To be My Bride.
You, Oh Jacob, I have lifted
And I have Forgiven
And set above kings.
I have paid a ransom for you
And cherished you
And Loved you with an Everlasting Love.
I build for you a palace,
Furnishing it with fountains,
And cedar for you to sit upon.
I have made infertile land bloom,
Deserts live, that once were dead.

All this I have made for you
And created in tenderness.
For Love has found you
And favoured you
And placed jewels and trinkets
About your neck.
Love has adorned you
And held you.
Kings will bow and bend low
In your presence,
For I, the Lord God, have favored you
And captured your soul.

You are Mine;
I have begotten you.
I choose you, Oh Israel, for My Bride.
Of all brides, I, the King, have chosen you,
And We have danced the Dance of Heaven
With all joy,
And hosts sing Our praises,
For I have lifted you
From a lowly place
To heights beyond you,
And I have Loved you.

Ah, My Bride, My love,
This is My wish for you.
O earth, I call to you
And My Words are not melodies
To your ears;
They are not music to you.
Look, I give you a lamp for your feet,
My Words, My Light, My Joy, My Peace.
Come, My Bride, the Bridegroom awaits you.

Lament of The Lover

My children, it is I, upon this Day of My Joy[1].
That I should be honoured this Day gives Me
joy.

I hear your prayers, My people. I can hear
you calling out of the wilderness and I, with the
Compassion of My Heart, will come and look
for you. My Heart must pierce you, My Heart
must become a part of you in order to envelope
you and teach you in the Ways of its Love. Love
pours from its inner depths into you, for it is for
you. Like the Shepherd I carry you, I lead you
to Good Pasture. It is the pasture of My Heart.
Look beyond your own lives at this time and see
this Heart that burns out of control, so much
Love it has for you.

But amid the joy and the Love there is Pain,
My little ones. I ask that you say a prayer of
consecration to Me on this Day of My Heart
and say it always, each day, each year of your life.
Do this and you will find Me. This is My Promise

to you. All of you who hear these Words of Love, be consumed by them for it is for them that you search. Look no further, search no further. These are the Words of comfort that you seek. Let them caress you, let them touch you, let you know them.

Hear, Oh children, hear this Great Heart beat its Love as it pumps in its depths to give you Love. This Vessel that empties itself in its Passion. Look to the great raging waters of the seas. See how in its anger that it rises to great heights. See its swell and its rise as it tosses everything in its path. It is like the Flames that burn within this Vessel of My Heart. Its Passion is its Love, its Passion is its Pain. Its Passion is you, My children.

Ah, little ones, how can I ever make you understand this Heart? I can find nothing upon this earth in which to show you its depth, its Treasures.

Contemplate Me, think Me and I will embroider the patterns of Wisdom upon your soul. I will etch the Understanding upon you. My Father shall draw you through this Gate which is Me. He will give you over to this Heart, into My Hands and I will tenderly care for all of your wounds. I will not see your sins, though they be many. I will only see the child that I have lost and longed for, that I have wept for.

But no, My people, I am a wounded animal. They have cut Me further and they have opened this Flesh. Those who say that they love Me have become the hunters that track Me down. They have traced My Footprints of Blood. They have found Me within My Church. My own are the enemies who hound Me without mercy. They are those who have taken vows that say they belong to Me. But they are not shepherds for I have not hired them. They are wolves in sheep's clothing who carry off My little lambs. Great shall be their reward for it shall be as though a great millstone were put around their necks and they were thrown into the deepest part of the ocean, these enemies of My Body.

Oh, My people, My people what have I done to you? What have I done to you that I should have deserved what you give to Me as Love? My Sorrow has engulfed Me on this Day of Joy and I cannot feel joy for My people are against Me and

55

not for Me. Those who are called Mine by the world are not Mine. Oh, My people, My people, what have I done to you? You have stripped Me naked and you have beaten Me with your lies. Yet My Treasure Houses still lie open and waiting for you to come and have your fill. The Lighted Lamp still burns in the darkness. The tomb is empty, My children, I am Risen and soon I will return as I have promised you. My Heart is given to great sadness in this time.

Some joy is within Me to see you within My Heart, My House, to be with Me. Will you give this wounded, hunted God a place to hide within your heart this day? A place of comfort and a place of love? Let Me sup with you and bide with you a little.

I Love you, My children, and I ask that you quash all evil within this world with simple Love. Find the broken and heal them with Love. Call them to My House, My Heart and renew their strength with the Love that I have given you and your strength and joy will be renewed in doing so. Find the darkness and shed My Light, find the uncomforted and comfort them. Find the spiritually dead and bring them back to life, find the sinners and show them forgiveness. I ask that My Love is intertwined with compassion, forgiveness, tolerance, obedience, willingness and a determination to win souls for Me. Do not get discouraged My little ones, for this is the evil one's weapon against you but let My hope be the lamp that you carry for it is a sure Light that never goes out.

On this Day of My Heart, I ask that all who work within it and all who come here and all who Love with My Love, I ask that you be renewed and revitalized in these Words for the way ahead is treacherous and in it lies many dangers for My children, My soldiers of the Light. As My Gift to you this Day, I shower My Love upon you for Love is the greatest Gift that I can give you because it is Me. Have you a gift for Me, My little ones?

¹ *Feast of the Sacred Heart.*

Charity's Flame

inspired by Jesus

Invest within me,
Oh Flame of Charity,
Thy Fire of Sweet Love,
That I might give love for Love,
And Thy Love only,
To give and give
And light Thy Fires in each heart
Ne'er to quell
Nor quench
In biting sin
But burn and burn
Until but dust be wrought
Of self.
No more to afflict
And blacken
And scourge
But dead to all
But Thy Love.

Ingrain in me,
Oh Flame of Charity,
A self same Love of all mankind.
That I might serve Thee only
And delight Thee
And caress Thy comely Lips
With smiles of joy
And cause happiness
To be Thy Sacred Lot.
For Thou art my Love
And only Thee can wrench from me
The darkness that I have spawned
The granite heart which is formed within me
And given over to the darkness.
And Thou wouldst fight and battle
And war to set me free
From the sin that I have fought so hard to keep.
Indwell in me,
Oh Flame of Charity,
And keep me in Thy stead
Safe and rescued
From the night which tears me forth
And grapples for my very soul.
In Thy Flame's Light

Do Thou couple me
That I may not flee
From terrors in the night
Whose arrows do me pierce
And wound me with their darkness
But wrest with me
'Til the day be done
And the battle won
And I am Thine
To serve Thee in Eternity.

From 'The Way'

The soul:

Love Him with every moment of your time; loving Him, embracing Him with love for He seeks a return of the Love that He has given us.

Run to Him with love for He thirsts for it. Be like a little child that runs to its mother with every new thing that it discovers. Let Him delight in you as you begin to discover The Way of His Heart. Thus you will realise that the Hermitage is being built on each moment that you share with Him and give to Him with a sincere heart, wanting to discover what He wants and doing it. Never forget that He is always there in the pain of dying to self, when the self wants its own way. In each second of the fight to overcome, He is there encouraging with many Graces and Love. All we have to do is take them.

Jesus:

In the depths of your spirit I will arise.
Come, calling to Me.

Do not fear, My dove.
The night is dark,
The journey long.
Much pain to be felt.
Do not fear losing control.
Be free;
Fly with Me on the Wings of Love.
Come, soar with Me
To pastures green.
The land of milk and honey
Awaits you, My dove.
Do not fret,
Do not worry,
Do not let self draw and tear.
Come, come, run, My Bride,
I, your All, am near.

The Soul:

Each time the self is overcome then the closer we allow Him to come to us. It is like a field that has never been used to grow anything on, a fallow field. First, the sods of earth must be removed in order to allow the plants to be placed in the earth and to grow without hindrance. The soil must be broken up and manured to help the plants grow.

All this involves much work and this is only the preparation. Nothing has been planted yet. We cannot hope to plant in soil that is already taken up with other plants that we cannot eat or will be of no benefit to us. These things that we have allowed to grow because of our selfish desires will choke the new plants if they are not removed.

My Jesus, my Love, You are all to me. Where has our Lovesong gone? Is it faded now? Am I lost from Your sight?

Where is Your smile for me? I do not see it anymore. I do not see Your Lips part in joy when You see me come to You. I do not feel Your Touch seed and grow and blossom and bear fruit within me.

Oh, Delicate Heart, that I love,
Come close to this little heart
This night.
I am cold without Your Fire
Within me.
I am feeling death,
For no Spirit leaps within me
No joy is mine to banquet in.
I love You, my Jesus, my beautiful God.

I am stricken, I am stricken.
I stand alone,
No cloak is about me.
Immersed in loneliness,
Engulfed in darkness.
My only cry is You, my God and my All.
They are about me, my enemies.
They put fear into the soul
That You have pledged Your Love for.
Oh Heart of Divine Fire,
Sublime Sweetness,
I take comfort in You.
And I love You.
I write Lovesongs to You.
But You are my joy, my Love.
How I would love You
If it were my joy to see You.

The Interlude of Darkness

1

Ambivalent thoughts,
Procured
By self:
To die or not to die.
For self in the darkness
Creates the scenario
Of life intermingled
With death.
The battle begins
In the interlude;
The waiting time,
The lull
Of Grace time, or not.
The blindness of the eyes – spiritual–
Encompassing
All
Said and done.
And the Dance
Has stopped.

No song,
No music.
And frenzied
And incapable
Of progress.
For My Hand
Has halted
The Song
To grow and fashion,
And design
The dancer.
I am the Dance.
I am the Song.

2
Play the darkness,
Play the silence.
And not a 'rest',
But a search;
A blindness.
The darkness weeps
And mourns
The sweetness.
And grief

Engulfs and binds,
And tries the steps
Of the Dance.
And without the Song
Is awkward,
Fumbling.
The dark night begins.
And to thee who would
Dance
Waiting in the darkness,
Forlorn,
Alone,
Grapple and battle.
For the ear attuned
Will hear the echoes
Of the Song,
Will see the image
Of the Dancer,
Smiling
Beckoning
Calling
Onward
On the spiral
And upward

And onward
The darkness calls.
And frenzied is the soul
Who calls
And sings My Song,
My Love.

3

Fear aside
The darkness,
Like a blade,
Will cauterise
And burn.
The seared soul
Will delight
And mourn
And give
And take
And win
And lose.
The dancer urging
Will slip the blade
Between flesh and spirit.
And with a "yes" from the dancer

Will cut
And tear
The rotted "flesh" -
The cancer of the soul.
And pain
And darkness
In the inner self
The controller, no more.

4
The self
Secluded
From all,
And blind, and deaf
And dumb,
Will not know
Of the Grace
Afforded in the darkness.
Self endeavours
To recover
By creating glitter
In the darkness.
And no created thing
Can comfort the dancer

For no Light
Is given.
For grief will sting
And I will wait,
And wait
For the acceptance of the dark time,
The Interlude.
I await
The giving in the darkness
For I wish
The purity of the soul.
And the flesh
Will hold
And chain
Entangled in the web,
Blind to all except self
Except its own want.

5
Soul, I call to thee.
Give Me the darkness,
Give Me the self,
And I will sing thee
A new Song

Of Love
Created only for thee
And thee alone.
I givest thou
My Love
In the washing
Of thy soul.
I bathe thy wounds
In Love.
I call to thee,
Lost soul,
To look upon Me
And gaze in wonder
At the sight,
Not to turn
And back away
And run
And hide again.
Do not hide thyself from Me
For thou hast captured
Love.
And Love has spent itself
On thee
And fleeing impurities

Wilt thou see.
And wilt thou not be Mine
In the "Interlude of Darkness"?
I Love you, children. Read these Words with your
heart and know what is in the 'darkest night'.

These Love Words

Like the rain I water you,
I nourish you.
My beloved children,
I would Love you,
I would give you My Heart
In these Words.
I have broken My Body
And I have shared it out among you
And Redeemed you through it.

In these Words, My people,
I place My sunshine
That you might be warmed in My Love.
For all that I have given you
Is My Love.
And poured out My Blood
And broken Body
To give you these Love Words.
In them I pour out My Spirit
Upon all who read them

And do them.
Each one who does My Father's Will
I will come to him
And My Father and I
Shall sup with him
And We shall live within him.
My people, dream this dream
For Me.
I Love you.

Whispers of Love

Patrick:

Jesus, the more I read the Lovesong the more I understand. Your Graces are the Song and You send it out to all Your children and in free will You must await its return for Your children to either accept it or deny it.

I see that it is a Song of great beauty but also of great sadness for so few return Your Song to You. So few are willing to take on The Dance.

Jesus:

My son, I Love you. Yes, now you begin to understand this Heart of Love. I cannot force My children to follow Me so I sing in whispers of Love within their hearts and I cry and lament as I am denied entry into their lives.

As I sing, many of My children recognise My calls and think it would be good to find Me. But then they feel the calls of the world once more and forget about Me. I am a God who is denied and rejected by My children every day.

No longer seen,
No longer heard;
The Dance goes on.
Looking and seeking
His partner of Love.
He cries for Love;
Love, He seeks.
No Love is heard
For Love is silent.
My beloved, My beloved,
Where are you?
Where have you gone?
I walk the pastures,
The hills and the dales
Seeking the Lovesong of My beloved.

Where have you hidden?
Why have you suppressed the Laments of Love?

Can the one who only offers darkness
In the guise of Light
Be so enchanting?
So that the Lovesong is lost
And not heard?

My beloved,
A Kingdom of Light I offer.
A Kingdom of Love.
It shall be one
And it shall be yours.
I am He who seeks and finds.
Come. Come beloved,
Answer My calls.

Built of Me

I will give thee My Grace,
I will give thee My Love,
I will give thee My Peace.
I shall astound men in thy sight
For I shall bring thee Myself
So that they may see My Love in thee.

I will take thee
And bring thee
The wealth of Graces
That I have preserved for Myself,
For thou art worthy
In My sight when thou dost My Will in earnest.

I am thy God,
Thou art My people
And I have planted a vineyard
In the heart of Israel
That I shall tend with My Love.
I give thee the keys to its door

To be its keeper.
Built of Me,
Thou shalt be strong
In the time of the sentencing of this world.
If thou hast walked the paths of saintliness
And done all things in My sight;
If thou hast been upright
Then thou shalt have all these things.

For I am the Giver of Life
And all who follow Me
Will have the reward of Life
In abundance.
I Love thee with My Heart.

And Thy Comeliness

inspired by Jesus

In Thy Godliness
Thou hast perfected me
And taken for Thyself
This soiled soul,
To eradicate
And dispel
The darkness from my soul.

Thy giving to me
In these Words
Is generous,
Proffered Love.
And I, in bewildered frame
Cannot pluck it
From Thy Hand
Nor yet refuse
For it is not mine
To renege
A Gift so pure

And sublime
That Thou givest me.

Oh that my love
Could move Thee
And caress Thee
And love Thee
In Thy Love.

Oh Creator,
Of which I am created,
These Words are nought
For Thee
And Thy comeliness.
But I know
That Thou dost Love
Them as though
They wert Thine own child
As I am.
Loving Father,
I gift Thee this small gift
Of my love.
Let Thy Countenance
Fall with favour on this world.

And stifle sin
And bodily wants
And Love
And Love
And Love
Until I be
Nothing but
All
For thee.

The Inner Sanctuary

This door is open, My children,
This door is open for you.
It is closed to no one
And it is the Inner Sanctuary
Of My Heart
And it is open for you.

Come and take My Love
And partake of My Presence.
I have created it for you.
Come and sup with Me
And be in My Company
Where I will give you My Love.
I will always give it to you
With an open Heart.
I Love you.
Jesus.

Love's Dream

My sons, I Love you.

We, the Three, are One
And I have called you
And exalted you among men.
My Work I have given you,
My teachings I have taught you.
Embrace Me
In your love.
Let nothing keep us apart
That I may allow you,
My two,
To see My Ways.
See My teachings
Are Wisdom itself.
They create in you
Cleanness
For your souls.
Imitate Me
Look to My teachings to you

For they are My Truth,
My Perfection of you.
Moulding, melting,
Filling,
Listening to you fulfil
Love's Dream.

I Love you.

Thou Art Mine Own

Perchance,
The thought in thee
Is Love, My son?
Perchance, it is My Love?
Touching thy little Heart
Enveloped
In Mine.

I, in My Love and thine,
Art touching thee
And thou art Mine own.

This Message came after I was thinking about
Jesus. I feel it shows Jesus in a 'playful mood.'

Abandon yourself deeper into Me

My little son, be aware of My Presence many times, for I am your Lord. I am your God. I have made you this way so that your only Love is Me. I gave Myself to you from the beginning and I continue to give Myself to you.

Your pain and sorrow, suffering and joy are Mine, for We are One. You are the soft reflection of Me and I delight in your soul. Abandon yourself deeper into Me. Look at Me, I am your only Peace.

Joy
Little one, joy -
Take it,
My Gift of Love to you.
My joy is to give you
My Love.
Let Me enhance you,
Enjoin you to Myself
For We are One.

You delight Me in your love
Of Me.
When all have abandoned Me
I find your heart open.
I Love you, My love.
Come.
I Love you.

Taste of Eternal Life

I will speak to you, My two sons, but I ask of you to believe the Words that I speak to you and do them. Do not let them just become Words in a book to you for they are very precious teachings that the world has never known for never before has it known My two witnesses of Love. I would never give you anything that I have not first experienced Myself.

When you feel the darkness descend upon you, as it must to test and call all of My children, then rely on and trust My teachings. Come and lay your heads on My Heart, which is reserved for you. Seek the comfort of My Heart in the Words that I have already prepared for you. It is your taste of Eternal Life.

I thank you that you have defended the Truth of My Words in these days. My Words that I give to you, I ask you to wear them as clothes for they are your protection and your Love. Let them flow with your own blood so that when you are wounded

then only My Truth shall flow from you.
Let Me speak Words of Love for you and to you,
My sons, for My Love spills over for you. Look!
Behold My Heart
It is for you, My sons.
It is given
For you are chosen
To witness My Love.
Though they pierce you
With insults
And scourge you with envy;
And persecute you
With lies,
You are
Because I Am.
And I will lift you high
To Me.
And I will lift you into
My Heart
Because you have heard
The Word of My Father
And do it.
I Love you.

The Great Fire

My children, I speak to you of a Profound Love that you must learn. Let it set your hearts on fire with the sheer depth of it. Do not let petty things stand in your way of learning it. It is My Love, children, a Love that overwhelms as it touches. It is sweet to the taste. It nourishes; it revitalises; it will abound within you.

The great Fire of it will burn and burn in its Sweetness, in its Fiery embrace, for it is My Sweet Wine that I give; it is My Blood.

Yes, My children, reach out for it, for I give it freely to you this day and, yes, it is the Love that My Francis was given. That is why I speak on this day of Great Love. Let it trickle into your soul and embellish each part of it - yes! even unto its deepest centre. Close your eyes and waste not time on selfish things, but step into what I offer.

Learn My Ways; learn what brings Me joy within you, for if you wish to learn, then I am your Teacher. How can salt be made to be salty again, when it has lost its taste? How can I make My Words, 'I Love you,' to mean again all of this that I speak? Oh children, look for this Love, for it is given freely to you. Let it be your joy; let it be your very life. Do not be afraid to enjoy its Fruits, whether in the dark times, or in the Light. Love is your joy. Include Me in your joy. I Love you.

The Road I Trod

inspired by Jesus

The dark night in abandonment led
My soul to where His Bosom bled.
I stepped out and called His Name,
Weary from the road I trod.
And then I saw Him with mine eye
And behold my soul did die.
For in Him I wanted no more
But Abandonment from my life.
Love's Head, I held upon my breast,
I cried out to Him,
'Burn me in Your Love'.
Now I'm forever lost.

This is no longer the night but it has become the
present moment and I have found Him within it.
This is where He dwells and if I seek Him, this
is where I will find Him. It seems that there is no
other time to find Him; He is always here, waiting.
There is gentleness and peace here for it exudes

from Him like a perfume. My hermitage is filled by
His Presence and His Hand touches my soul.
My Love has entered the thicket.
He has joined me in my house.
I searched for Him and could not find Him
But He waited for me.
I have climbed the hill
And found Him.
He touches me and my house is razed
By His Love.
He has come from I know not where,
But He has come.
My Love is content.
His Love is in His Breath
That He breathes on me.
His Love is in His Words.
I am captured by His Love.
My heart is content in Him.
His Heart is my Hermitage
Perfumed by His Love.

Dying to Self

Listen,
Listen to the call of Love,
Call, that echoes and draws.
Come, My love,
Let Me draw you.
See Me in the dawn,
In the shadows
That draw the day forth.

Sing, sing, child,
Feel now,
Feel the draw within,
The call.
It is I, your Love.

We, together, are One.
Love.

Come, dance,
Dance, My love,

On the strings of Love.
My caresses pull, draw,
Closer.
The self cries out,
Lancing pain,
Drawn flesh stripped
In death,
And emerging freedom, Love.
Come,
Feel the knowledge,
Find freedom, My Love.

The unknown, yet known;
Fear, yet freedom;
And weakened self dies.
Emerging freedom found,
Soaring into Me.
The unknown,
Its silken threads,
A joy,
Ever drawn,
Flying now,
Into freedom.

E-mail:
To obtain general information from the House of Prayer:
info@thetwopatricks.org
If you wish to have pro-life printing done, such as posters,
postcards, Message Books, etc., please use:
printroom@thetwopatricks.org
If you wish to place an order, such as books, pamphlets,
Holy Oil, Holy Water, images, Newsletters, please use:
orders@thetwopatricks.org
Website:
www.thetwopatricks.org